Table of Contents

Dedication

First and foremost, I would like to thank God for giving me the courage and strength to face the challenges I have encountered along my path. Thank you for allowing me to focus on what is essential while reassuring me that you already have my life figured out, even if I don't understand. May my story bless someone else as they travel through life.

To my family and friends, your support and reassurance have been a constant need in my life. I genuinely thank you for the continuous prayers, words of encouragement, phone calls, text messages, visits, petitions, as well as financial support. I have received an overwhelming amount of support, too many to list. Those of you who have genuinely and wholeheartedly supported me know who you are.

To my fellow officers in law enforcement who showed unwavering support through this challenging time, many of you have stuck by me as a brother, not only in blue. Regardless of the outcome, I will never forget the unconditional support.

Last but not least, to the brothers of Kappa Alpha Psi Fraternity Incorporated, thank you for embracing me at all times, but especially at a time when I needed it the most. Mere words cannot express what your support means to me. Yo!

~Cameron Brewer

Prologue

The game of life is so close to sports that everyone should be considered an athlete. Whether you are training to be an athlete, store manager, or even a reasonable person in general, you will experience adversity, set-backs, wins, losses, and what seems like insurmountable obstacles along the way. Every aspect of your life helps to define who you are today. Everyone is here for a purpose no matter what it may be. It is up to you to find that purpose and fulfill it.

My name is Cameron Brewer, and this is my story. Police officers come from different walks of life, but I wanted to allow you to walk with me along my journey. Initially, the goal of my career was never to be a police officer. I would have never guessed in a million years I would be here right now. The truth is, I am, and I know

God has ordered my steps to walk this path for a reason. This book gives a chance for my voice to be heard. By the time you reach the last page, I hope that you see the man behind the badge. Take a moment to ask yourself the simple question that you find there.

1st Quarter-The Foundation

I grew up in a "normal," middle class, loving family. There was my mom Jean, dad James, sister Nikki, brother Jimmy, and my brother Brian, who I didn't get to grow up with because we had different mothers, but he is STILL MY BROTHER.   I never wanted for anything growing up as my parents somehow found a way to give us whatever we needed, and then some.

Though each of us siblings was two years apart, we had very different relationships. I was the oldest, and Jimmy was the youngest. Of course, growing up, he was that pesky brother who always wanted to be in my room, but as the big brother, you know that I was too cool for that. My sister and I being that we were closer in age, seemed to tolerate each other more. Even with all that said, we all had an unbreakable bond as siblings from an early age. As we grew older, our parents divorced and Nikki, Jimmy and I moved with my mother from Chicago to

Champaign. With each year, our relationships grew closer, as my mom worked to provide for us, and we never wanted for anything.

Growing up, we had plenty of friends and always seemed to have a lot going on. My "crew" in high school was tighter than stitches. We called ourselves the Bad Boyz- Kevin Williams, Terence Smith, Terrence Williams, Carlos Spinks, Kentra Kimbrough, Dan Barham, Rashidi Overstreet (rest in Heaven) and me. We had the world's greatest high school intramural basketball team, let us tell it. We challenged our high school team, but it never happened. My relationship with those guys was so strong that we did EVERYTHING together. We all came from different sides of town but were the best of friends. Myself, Terence, and Terrence went on to play high school football together. The bond we ALL shared is TRULY for life. We had a lot in common, and we all loved sports. Bad Boyz 4 Life!!!

I remember spending the night at Kentra's house often. His mama didn't play! He had to make sure all of his chores were complete before we could do anything, which meant when I spent the night, his duties became my chores as well. I thank her for that to this day because it helped to reinforce responsibility. Kentra laughs to this day when we reminisce about that. Reco had the same type of expectations at his house. He had a newspaper route, so we always had to take care of that first. That made me want a newspaper route. My first ever job I learned from him. There were so many opportunities to learn from my high school friends and their families.

Playing high school football was epic. Riding on the bus to away games was a blast. Terrence's mom always made sure we had plenty of food. I used to eat some of his sandwiches, even on the way to the game.

My number was 78 in high school, and my best friend at the time was Terence Smith, and he wore the number 87. We would even dress alike on some days. Crazy how a childhood friend can stay in your life forever. Terence is now the father of my niece Kim and nephew T'Andre.

As a kid, playing sports was a way of life for me. Football, basketball, baseball, you name it, I have always played team sports. After high school, I went on to play college football at MacMurray College in Jacksonville, Illinois. Before going to college, I had never lifted a weight in my life. When I got there, I was embarrassed because being a big guy; they expected me to lift a lot. I couldn't even lift the bar.

Coach Frey was like a father to me. He would get me up at 4 am so I could get in some good strength and conditioning training one on one. I got stronger, pretty quick. He was like my father away from home and helped to make me the man I am today, and I am thankful for his investment and belief in me. Coaches Foley, Protz and Schrage also believed in me from day one. I was surrounded by people who cared about me.

My circle of friends was amazing and included Ben, E.C., Johnny, Marlo, Juice, A.D., Scotty, Skinner, The Kern Brothers, France, Dalke,

Koker, Marty, Frank, Jeremiah, as well as many other friends and teammates. I was even part of a rap group! The DOG POSSE…lol. Myself, Marcius, Paul, Ben, A.D., and Phil (rest in heaven) used to set up a little makeshift studio in our dorm room to rap. Christy used to even talk on the songs. Those were the days. I had several other friends that impacted my life like Gina, Julie, Shonta, Maureen, Jennifer B., Jen C., Rhonda, and Heather.

I remember showing up to college and meeting teammates from all walks of life. Being born in Chicago and living there and Champaign, Illinois, I was used to being around people from larger cities who were comfortable with all races. Having a chance to connect with teammates with a hometown population of 200 people in it was a huge culture shock for me.

MacMurray College was a blessing for many reasons. I majored in Criminal Justice because I wanted to become a Juvenile Probation Officer. I wanted to help juveniles stay out of trouble while holding them accountable.

Being an athlete who stood 6'3" and weighed 315 pounds, I was faced with many challenges. The college was welcoming to ALL its students; however, I remember going to the stores with my non-black teammates and being frustrated because of how I was treated. What gave me gratification was my teammates who didn't look like me taking a stand against racism and standing up to those people who treated me differently because of the color of my skin. Team sports sees no color, race, or origin. I was thankful for the opportunity to play college football with a group of guys like this.

I excelled at sports, winning such awards as First Team All-Conference my Junior and Senior Year, Pre- Season All-American my Senior year, Team Offensive Captain, and Offensive Lineman of the Year (Conference). Achieving these accolades was exhilarating.

My most memorable times as a college athlete was going to the local schools and reading books to kids. It was such a cool project, and it made all of us feel like we were famous people. A picture of me reading to kids was not only on the front page of the local newspaper, but the college decided to use it as the cover of their Book of Majors the following school year to send to prospective students. That was truly special to me, I was 19 years old, and this made me feel like a celebrity. The smiles on the kids' faces were priceless. Those moments were, by far the best of my college career.

As my undergraduate years came to a close and graduation day arrived, the bonds I made, and friendships formed were all that mattered to me. Playing football all over the world and even studying in Europe, helped with my overall growth. I graduated and truly felt that I became a Man during my college years. I was confident that I developed a strong foundation to tackle this game called life.

After graduation, I went back to Champaign to start my professional career. My first job out of college was at a state-funded facility called Cunningham   Children's Home. CCH was a residential facility for kids who removed from their families due to being physically, emotionally, and sexually abused. The cottage I worked in was all boys ages 12-16. This job was challenging, but I felt as though I was helping to provide stability and structure to kids whose lives needed this very thing. The kids were at times heavily medicated and very much reliant on their scheduled doses. This job was rewarding for so many reasons and made me feel like I was giving back to society because I treated them like they were my children. The goal was that they wanted to be better young men because they felt as though someone cared about them, which gave them hope.

While working there, I was able to meet other men and women who genuinely loved kids. Vernon, Larry, Mike, Tonia, and Mikki were great mentors for me. I became very close with Mikki Johnson. We seemed to hit it off instantly and became the best of friends. He had the same drive I had, same background (played football in college) and more importantly, the same love for kids. We worked together seamlessly, and it became apparent that we were definitely on the same team. I don't think Mikki can imagine the significant impact he has had on my life.

After working at Cunningham for two years, I got the opportunity of a lifetime. I received a call from an old childhood friend regarding working for the Don Moyer Boys and Girls Club. I was hired as the Unit Director at the Boys and Girls Club in Champaign, Illinois. This opportunity was an absolute dream come true. The Boys and Girls Club, "The Positive Place for Kids," was an after-school program that catered to at-risk youth. My job was to oversee the daily operation of the club and maintain the upkeep of the entire facility. We serviced approximately 200 kids per day, Monday through Friday. I was hired to take the place of local legend Jackie Vonner, whose shoes I could never fill, but I hoped to enter this position with the heart to make a difference in the lives of kids. Upon his exit and my arrival, it was clear to him that I had a passion for positively impacting the lives of youth. He mentored me while I took on this enormous task. Without Jackie taking me under his wings, I could never have affected as many kids as I did at the club. He bridged the gap because he had been there for so long. He assured them I was trustworthy.

Our program had different components that we offered to keep kids engaged. There was a teen program, physical fitness, games, arts and crafts, tutoring, and mentoring, to name a few. The Club played a significant role in the development of the kids in the inner city. I would not have been able to do this job without the Program Director- Denisha Tate and Teen Coordinator- Donte Lotts. Denisha was a student at the University of Illinois and had access to hundreds of volunteer groups. Donte' "Tay-Luv" was our Teen Program Coordinator and was WELL respected and deeply rooted in the community, more importantly, the inner-city. We made a phenomenal team.

During my time at The Club, we mentored over a thousand kids. Many of the kids came to the Club because their parents attended the Boys and Girls Club when they were younger, while others came because we were the closest thing to a parent figure that they had. Of course, we all had our favorites. It's funny because one of my favorites, Markisha Brinson (Motton) now lives in Houston and we talk all the time. It makes me so proud to see her with a family and employed by Harris County. She is now able to give to society because The Club gave to her. This job was gratifying on so many levels. There was one person who oversaw the financial side of the club, and I wanted to be able to do that as well. The only thing that separated us was a master's degree.

Obtaining a masters degree was something I wanted because I felt it could open more doors and allow me to reach even more kids. These feelings catapulted me into the search for a master's program that would suit me. After researching different colleges and universities, I decided I was going to step out on faith and move to Houston, Texas, to attend Texas Southern University to pursue a Master's Degree in Public Administration.

2nd Quarter-The Move

Attending a historically black college was an educational opportunity that I felt would have a significant impact on my life. I felt Texas Southern University was my best option because Houston was such a thriving city, and it's where I would stay when I was done earning my degree. My family was pretty surprised that I wanted to move so far away, considering the majority of my family was in Illinois and Louisiana. I had been to Houston one time, and that was to register for classes. I didn't have relatives or friends in the city, but I did not let that influence my decision. My mom, dad, and brother rode with me in my Ford Expedition, pulling a trailer with what little belongings I had 16 hours to Houston, Texas. They bought one-way tickets home after we unloaded my trailer. I moved here with $2000.00, no job, a truck (not paid for) and a new apartment. Once we were done unloading my things, I drove my family to the airport. Upon arrival at the airport, my mother was so upset that she would be leaving her oldest son in a massive city that she got out of the truck and did not even say goodbye. I knew it wasn't out of anger, and she knew her firstborn child had just moved across the world. My dad and brother gave me encouraging words before they departed.

As I left the airport, it was a sunny day in August, but the strangest thing happened. The sun was shining bright, but it was pouring down rain in certain areas. In all honesty, I was a little shook by this as it was uncharted waters. I had never seen anything like this in my life. This sudden move was a leap of faith for me, but I was ready. I knew I wanted to impact youth, and I felt getting a master's degree would afford me a better chance. I registered for classes at Texas Southern University to start my master's program.

Being in a big city without family support, I knew that I needed a job because I didn't have money. Any employment would do at this point. The second day I was there, I wandered south on Interstate 45 and found Almeda Mall. I walked into Foley's (now Macy's) and asked the first person I saw that worked there if they were hiring.

I was employed on the spot working loss prevention.

Being employed was great, considering that I had just moved here two days earlier. It wasn't much pay, but I was grateful. I didn't work there long because I was already homesick and was informed I couldn't be off during the holidays due to it being busy in loss prevention. I worked the job as long as I could and then eventually started substitute teaching. Being a substitute teacher worked well because it helped me become more acclimated to the city.

When it was time to register for classes, I didn't know what to expect. The very first day, they dropped me from my classes stating some of the required paperwork was not submitted. I was visibly confused because I had no idea what to do. I guess the perplexed look on my face was so obvious, a male student looked at me and inquired what was wrong. I explained the situation as he smiled and said, "Everything will be fine man; it's always like this." He introduced himself as Ron Burnett and welcomed me to TSU and Texas. Ironically, we were in the same graduate program. He was the very first person I met at Texas Southern. Ron was a member of

Kappa Alpha Psi Fraternity Incorporated and hailed from Fort Worth, Texas. The willingness to help me get acclimated to Houston was incredible to me. He showed me around the city and even took me to his hometown. He pretty much taught me the ropes. I was so thankful for meeting him and the help and guidance he provided to me as a perfect stranger said a lot about his character and his southern hospitality.

As we made it through our degree program, Ron and I became pretty close, and he introduced me to his line brothers (Bernard, Will, Terrence, and Don). Ron, Bernard, and I hung out a lot. This friendship helped me get to know more about them, the city of Houston, places to go and things to do. The more I hung out with these guys, we became closer, and I grew more interested in Greek life. I didn't know much about fraternities at all, but I remembered my best friend Mikki and I talked about pledging Omega Psi Phi. I thought all big football guys pledged Omega. That proves I had a lot to learn about Greek life. I started to question Ron about Kappa Alpha Psi (ΚΑΨ). He told me to do my research on all of the fraternities and see which one fit me best. After doing so, I knew that becoming a Kappa was for me. After a "process," I became a member of Kappa Alpha

Psi Fraternity Incorporated. Becoming a member was special to me because I had a unique brotherhood with other progressive and professional males.

As I continued through the graduate program, I met classmates that were established in different careers. I started substitute teaching while going to classes at night. During these night courses, I met Janice, who was a director at MHMRA (Mental Health and Mental Retardation Authority). She was in a few of my classes and found out that I was looking for a steady job. She hired me to be a case manager on her team. Things seemed to be falling into place for me as I was now tasked with coordinating services for 25 clients who were mentally ill. I had to make visits all over the city, so this was perfect considering I was so new to Houston, and this helped me learn about different parts of the city.

While working at MHMRA, I met Christopher. We were assigned office mates, and like Ron, we hit it off well. He also welcomed me to Houston and was helpful in my learning my way around. I was pleased with my move and had met some genuine people. While work was rewarding at MHMRA, I knew it was not going to be a career job, but it was beneficial for my transition while helping me through graduate school.

One evening I was invited to a happy hour where I met Sandy, who was the Associate Director of Residential Life and Housing at the University of Houston. After talking to her, she encouraged me to apply as an Area Coordinator. I would be overseeing the resident assistants. I was able to impact college students and provide them with guidance and mentorship. Me being new to the university, my top R.A Souzi, was my right hand! She supported me, and we worked great together. Without her, I would not have been successful at this job. Working for U of H was a cool job; I lived in the residence hall as part of my salary. I was just happy to be supporting the growth of college students.

While I worked at the U of H residence halls as a coordinator, I started noticing that many of my cohorts had made the transition into education and were principals. That became intriguing, and the thought of becoming a principal of an elementary school piqued my curiosity. I graduated with a master's degree, and the time had come for me to put my plan into place.

3rd Quarter- Educating the Community

As I set out to take on the next quarter of my life, I had already set a goal, which was to be principal of an elementary school. To do this in the state of Texas, you have to teach for five years. I set my sights on working in the Houston Independent School District, seeing that it had some of the most at-risk students in the city. Another desire I had was to work in Houston's historic Fifth Ward. During this time, it was a very low-income community, and there was a shortage of positive African American male role models in the community.

Since my degree was in criminal justice, I had to enroll in an alternative teacher certification program and get hired by a school. Dr. Gloria Nash was the principal at Isaacs Elementary, located in Kashmere Gardens, and I am forever indebted to her because she was the first to allow me to teach children.

During my first year at Isaacs, I had such amazing support from the staff and the parents. Students like Marquell and Stephen were very busy, to say the least, and they, along with several other students, became "my special friends." What these kids needed was a little more guidance, a little more patience, and a lot of love and support during the school day. Their mothers, Ms. Tamika, and Ms. Patricia gave me the green light to mentor these boys and to treat them like they were my own. These relationships made education so fascinating, and that was important to me. I was driven harder to do the best I could as a positive male role model and educator.

Being a black male teacher in this community, many students saw me as a father figure. My kids' parents often told me that I was the only male figure in their lives. That made me realize the value of the role I was playing in their lives. Being a teacher was such an essential job to me, and there was one question that kept me up at night, "How can I reach ALL of them?" That question inspired me to step into Isaacs daily and give a 150% to my students because I knew that I could not be just another man that let them down.

Becoming a successful teacher doesn't happen by accident. It takes collaboration and a willingness to learn yourself continually. My mentor teacher Mrs. Ryans, Ms. Gilford, Ms. Durio, Ms. Sims (rest in Heaven), Mrs. Adams, Mrs. Williams, and Mrs.Rodriguez all made me the teacher that I became. I'm sure there are a few more that I may have forgotten to mention, but all played a part in my drive to be the best that I could be for my students.

The following school year, my principal moved me to third grade, which was a state testing grade level. I was excited about the challenge and even got some of my same students from the previous year. Having some of my old students was great because I already had a positive rapport with the students and their parents. I was natural in this role that parents enrolling their kids into the school were requesting my class for their students. I was fortunate enough to win the Teacher of the Year Award in my second year of teaching. I had a hold on the community, and the kids bought into me and learning. It was popular to be in Mr. Brewer's class. My kids would tell you, "He's so hard on us, but we love him, and he loves us." I gave my kids the mentality that we had to work twice as hard as other kids who lived across town. Some of my kids couldn't clean their uniforms, so I took them home to wash them. If they needed supplies, I bought them. When extra tutoring was required, I would meet them at the local library on the weekend. Whatever it took, I did. I gave them a bedtime and used to call some of them to make sure they were in bed. If there was one thing, I learned from this experience is that you never know the circumstances that a family may be experiencing, and if you can do one small thing to impact their life to make learning a little easier, it would go a long way.

I had such a special bond with all of my students. My classroom secretary was Alancia. She stayed on top of all of my paperwork to be passed out. I didn't even have to tell her what needed to be passed out. She came into class daily and did her job with pride while being a great student, which made my job as a teacher easier. Jaylan and Julia were sisters. Jaylan was older, so I taught them in different years, and they were both superstars. Their grandmother, Ms. Watson, was our "Reading- Success for All Coordinator," so it was apparent they were my reading, as well as my classroom stars. Their names were always on my "Brewer's Best" board for repeatedly scoring high on their assessments.

One student that I worked hard to build a relationship with was named Devon. He was a pretty special kid, and one of my biggest challenges. It was evident that this kid wanted to do well, but he was not motivated. Something great that he had going for him was his mother, Ms. Wallace. She was a single mother and put her heart and soul into his academic success. I used to meet them on the weekends, after school, or whenever we could to help get him up to speed. I had a real bond with him and remembered preparing for the TAKS test (Texas Assessment of Knowledge and Skills), which was the state's mandated test before the STARR Test. I challenged him to do well, and when the results came back, he received commended performance in math. I was so proud of him, and I loved him not only because he believed in me and what I had instilled in him, but because he believed in himself. His mother was special to me as well because she cared so much for her son, and it was truly evident. Sometimes mothers of African American students are given a bad rap from our school systems. Ms. Wallace, Ms. Leday, and Ms. Drumgo were some of the best mothers with whose students I worked collaboratively to create a strong home-school partnership to support the students.

Another student, Patrick, was a pretty cool kid as well. He and his mother were special to me. I was tough on Patrick because I wanted him to do well. I used to tell him all the time, "I'm hard on you now, so the police won't have to deal with you later." Those conversations about this remain in my mind to this day. Dailon and Areonna were two more favorites. They were sister and brother to Stephen, who I had taught, in addition to Keyshawn. They were an amazing family. As you can see, I took teaching seriously, and my love for kids and their overall development was unwavering.

A very vivid memory I can see as if it were yesterday is picture day one year. One student, Demond, came to school and gave me his backpack. He told me that his mother sent hair clippers to school for me to cut his hair. I was surprised because my head was bald so I wasn't sure what she wanted me to do to his hair, so I called her. She said, "I trust you, Mr. Brewer, please make him look nice." That was all I needed to hear. I started the class lesson, grabbed a trash bag, tore a hole in it for his head, sat him in front of me and cut his hair while I taught the lesson, and I didn't skip a beat. When I finished, I sent him to the restroom to wash up, and he came back beaming. He ended up with a very nice haircut, even if I do say so myself. Demond was so proud of how he looked for picture day because it showed when he returned from the restroom smiling.

I was everything to them. I pulled teeth, cut hair, cleaned uniforms, whatever it took for my kids to achieve success, I did. I LOVED education. They needed me, and I needed them because they gave me a sense of purpose. They trusted me, and I challenged them to be the best that they could be. My kids always did great on not only state testing, but overall academic success.

I was fortunate enough to have a partner who taught 3rd Grade with me, Steven Eaton. Eaton was my brother from another mother. He was a former athlete like myself, a member of Omega Psi Phi Fraternity, and most of all LOVED kids as I did. I had never worked so closely with a teacher who was so much like myself. We quickly became the best of friends, and our kids in third grade knew they had two influential male teachers who cared about them, and we assured them they could come to us with any challenge that they encountered.

As the years went on, my LOVE for education and my kids became more and more evident. I became closely involved with our school improvement plan, and I was genuinely interested in keeping our kids and community safe. Our neighborhood was becoming more dangerous as I heard the stories of the kids discussing the horrible things they faced walking to and from school. Our area was so bad; we had a school district police officer, Officer Jones, assigned to our campus. We talked all the time about safety and security. I became more interested in keeping the school and community safety because I knew that it would be more and more challenging to teach my students if they didn't feel safe. My kids continued to do well, but my heart was starting to become more serious about their long-term safety and security. One day, Officer Jones said, "Brewer, you should become a cop." I replied, "Are you crazy?   I don't even like cops, man. Police have always mistreated me, and I can't see myself doing that." Jones assured me that I could bring my unique personality into the career and have a positive impact on our community. Once he told me that, I began to become more and more serious about this and started to ask questions daily about the job. To make a long story short, I enrolled in the Houston Community College Police Academy.

The following school year, I taught from 8 am to 3 pm and attended the academy from 5 pm to 10 pm for the next nine months. I no longer wanted to be an elementary school principal; I wanted to serve my community in a more hands-on role and make it safer for the kids I served. I remember my last day as a teacher, and I had graduated from the police academy and secured a job in law enforcement. To this day, I still talk to many of my students. It makes me feel old, but it's great to see who these kids have become and to know that I played a role in their growth, maturity, and to them becoming contributing members of society. I cried so hard leaving the kids behind because teaching them had become such an integral part of my life, but the time had come for me to protect the community and help make their lives better as a whole.   My next mission, that of protecting the people seemed to be an impossible task, but it was a calling that I answered.

4th Quarter-
Protecting the Community

I have always been a protector by nature. Being in education, I valued the lives of our innocent youth and became intentional about how to help ensure student safety. I started to become more and more interested in how we secured our school and the specific plans in place in case of an emergency. As a result, I left education and started in school district policing. I felt this way the best transition into law enforcement, due to me spending the last eight years in education.

My first full-time law enforcement job was with the Spring Independent School District Police Department. I started training at Dekaney High School, which had received media attention for lunchroom riots. Working in this capacity was a challenge. It was merely crowd control, and in my opinion, the limitations on what law enforcement could do in schools to positively impact student safety made it tough to police. I went from Dekaney to Westfield High School. While I enjoyed Westfield, I was still limited in what police actions we could take. Due to the lack of "police work" I could do, I became active with the football team. I remember watching the movie **End of Watch**, and I was not able to identify with the characters due to the limitations affiliated with school district policing. When I say limitations, I mean, before you can take any police action, school administration needed to be included and on board with the decision to pursue criminal charges or not if this was a "star athlete," good luck on following through with any charges. Not that everyone should be taken to jail or charged with a crime, but schools should be a haven for our children and to allow a culture of outright criminal activity to take hold of a school is negligent.

After almost a year of working for the Spring ISD Police Department, a new, larger department, Cypress Fairbanks ISD Police was starting and promised to have more opportunities. I made the transition to Cypress-Fairbanks, and I was assigned to Cypress Springs High School and loved it. I worked under then Principal Fanning, who was very serious about the protection and security of the school. Colette Vallot, Clay Smith, Mark Smith, Marshall Caplin, and the late Mrs. Cahee were an amazing administrative team that had a good pulse of the school. I worked with Officer Brown, who was also a former teacher. In my opinion, we worked well together. Officer Berryman worked next door at Hopper Middle School, but she helped us at Springs and brought a much-needed female dynamic to our team policing efforts. We would not have been successful without her.

While this was a great experience, I remained adamant about wanting to do traditional police work. I wanted to serve and protect the community on a larger scale, so I contemplated applying for the Texas Department of Public Safety (DPS) and started the application process. The problem was, they needed all original documents (birth certificates, etc.). I had copies of everything, so I had to produce authentic paperwork. I contacted my mother via text to ask her if I was born in Cook County or DeKalb County in Chicago. I let her know that I needed to order a birth certificate online. There was no response. I texted my dad, same thing, no response. As I got off work that day, my mother called me and asked me to come to her house. I thought it was strange since I had been trying to contact her. As I walked in the door, I could see her sitting on the couch sobbing. I didn't know what was wrong, so I started to console her. She just kept saying, "I'm so sorry, Cam, I'm so sorry." Finally, through the sobbing, she uttered, "James is not your father." I was numb, confused, devastated, betrayed, and most of all, hurt. I couldn't believe what I was hearing. It didn't seem real. James was the man I had known as my father for the last 40 years. After more conversation, she explained that she did not have much information about my biological father other than the fact that the last thing she knew he was a police officer in Washington D.C., this floored me. I couldn't believe what I was hearing. At age 40, I was hearing that my dad was not my dad. I was upset with my entire family because it appeared that everyone knew except Jimmy. I was truly devastated. The man I thought was my father, James Brewer Sr. took full responsibility for me and treated me as if I was his child. I have so much love for this man, and I owe my knowledge about being a man and my instincts to him. Anyone can father a child, but a MAN takes care of his children. James Brewer, Sr., you are a man, and I have so much respect for you. My wanting to know my biological father was not a reflection of you as a dad; I just needed to know.

My mom, dad, sister, Uncle Charles and Gina helped me begin the search to locate my biological father. With the help of my family, I was able to locate him, but he wanted nothing to do with me. I just wanted to know who he was if I had other siblings, and even more importantly, my medical history. I'm so thankful to his sister

Sharon and his Aunt Augustine, for being open to talking to me. They helped to shed some light on several questions I had concerning my birth father and a half of a family I had no idea existed for 40 years.

This information threw me for a loop. I was deeply hurt by not knowing this years ago, and I wanted to getaway. It's as though I needed to reset. I decided to apply for the Seattle Police Department. Like Houston, I didn't know anyone there and had never been, but I was ready to sell my house and relocate. I flew out to Seattle, had an appointment with an apartment locator and scheduled everything. The next day I tested for the Seattle Police Department and scored a 77%. I needed 80 %, so I was disqualified. While I was devastated, I knew it was not to be. I was running because I was hurt. I needed to face the hurt and move on with life. I realized that my purpose of making the community safer for the former kids I taught, their parents, and the city of Houston was far from done.

Back in Houston, there was a push for me to make an impact on serving and protecting my community. While working for a school police entity was rewarding, I knew that my heart was pulling me to make a difference in the community. I decided to apply to Harris County Precinct 4 and the Harris County Sheriff's Office. Precinct 4 gave me a call first. I learned a lot there and was fortunate enough to learn the Harris County system.

On the night shift, I had a great team with Deputies Howard, Paige, Jenkins, King, Denson, Martinez, and Malek. They were my brothers. We went through so much together and supported one another. At the time, Sgt. Bloomfield, Sgt. Sam, LT Lowry, and Sgt. Harrah were our leaders. I must say, I was treated well by all of them. They treated me respectfully at all times. I wanted to serve and protect, and that's what I was able to do. Our busiest contract was MUD (municipal district) 200, which was the Ella and Kuykendahl area. You name it; we dealt with it, shootings, stabbings, carjacking, aggravated assault, DWI, and domestic violence were prevalent. I vividly remember one specific call that I dealt with along with four other deputies and a supervisor. We received a call that a man was naked and was under the influence of PCP. The call came in from a concerned girlfriend who witnessed them smoking "wet" (PCP). Upon arrival, we were able to locate the two gentlemen.

One of the males, who was completely naked, complied with our commands to get on the ground and allowed himself to be handcuffed. The other male suspect wanted no part in dealing with law enforcement. After several commands to stop walking away from us so we could identify him, a physical struggle ensued. It took four of us to attempt to get him under control and cuff him. His strength was unbelievable as he was going through what is called "excited delirium." Excited Delirium is exhibited when someone is high on PCP and has supernatural strength and high pain tolerance. While on the ground, I was responsible for moving his right arm closer to his other arm to handcuff him. Safely restraining this suspect took four officers and three sets of handcuffs. The suspect would not stop resisting, and a taser was deployed several times. The taser did not affect the suspect. We were able to request EMS who finally arrived on the scene and received permission from their supervisor to administer a "special" sedative which after the second injection, the suspect was sound asleep in less than five seconds. That was the hardest struggle I had ever faced with a suspect. I was thankful I had the support of the other three officers and EMS. Working the south-central side of Precinct 4 was like a dream come true. After a couple of years at Precinct 4, I made a lateral transfer to the Harris County Sheriff's Office. Each move I made was for progression and more opportunity. Going from school district policing to the Harris County Sheriff's Office was a well-traveled journey. I was a sheriff deputy, and this gave me access to all of the resources I could ever need. After spending time training with my Field Training Officer, FTO Campbell, I was ready to hit the streets on my own.

Starting on nights, I worked closely with Deputies Aranda and Fry. I learned so much from them so fast. I enjoyed working the streets with K-9 Handler Nolan, Nash, Herdon and FTO's Perry and Burgess. HCSO was so fast-paced! We were busy all the time, but I loved it. I took pride in responding to calls and problem-solving different situations. After a few months, I moved to the day shift. This was the beginning of a whole new side of my law enforcement career. I quickly befriended Deputies Carter and Jones. The three of us became inseparable and answered almost all of our calls together. We readily backed each other up on calls. We all worked in "C" beat but would often run calls in different beats due to a large number of calls coming in through the dispatcher whenever we were needed. Our sergeants never bothered us too much because they knew we were hard workers. I just flat out loved to work. We all did. That's why we were so close. We were brothers and had been through so much together. I can't count the number of fatalities, major accidents, or dangerous calls we handled together.

One day, a call dropped in the "A" beat. It was a welfare check, but it had been holding for almost 40 minutes. The call was holding so long that a sergeant came across the radio and said, "Can we get a unit to answer this welfare check, it has been holding for over 30 minutes?" I was assigned to "C," along with Carter and Jones. I responded to the welfare check because I was available, and Carter and Jones got on the call slip to back me up. In reading the call, the wife stated she wanted us to meet her down the street from the residence because she was concerned about the behavior of her husband. Jones sent me a message to make sure I read and understood the comments. Carter did the same. We were always on the same page. We arrived down the street from the residence and met with the wife. She explained that her husband was acting erratically with their newborn baby. The mother had the child with her, so no one aside

from the husband was in the house.
We asked if there were weapons in the house,
and she replied, "Yes, but they are locked up."
We advised her to stay where she was. Carter,
Jones, and I walked up to the house, and we
realized the front door was open. That was not a
good sign. As we got closer, we noticed a wet
substance all over the wood floor in the living
room. I announced myself and called for the male
to talk to us. We did not see him downstairs, so
we walked into the house. Jones went in the
farthest, near the kitchen. Carter went to the
center corner of the living room, and I was near
the entrance. All three of us were in good tactical
position with a proper angle on the stairwell. As I
called for the resident, Jones whispered, "Hey
man, I hope this isn't the guy on this picture. He is
huge!!" Jones was referring to a good-sized,
buffed gentleman in a picture. I continued to call
for the resident, and he finally answered from
upstairs. I told him I was Deputy Brewer, and I just
wanted to talk to him. I explained his wife was
concerned. He yelled out in a strange voice,
"WHO IS THAT?" I repeated, "Deputy Brewer, I
just want to talk to you." Moments later, we heard
a pop-pop sound. I remember looking over at
Carter and Jones and asking, "Is this
motherfucker shooting at us?" Next, the suspect

who was still upstairs began to shoot an AR-15 at us through the ceiling.

Rounds were flying from everywhere, and we had no idea where exactly they were coming from. Jones got on the radio and announced, "Shots fired!" We began to retreat and make an attempt to get out of the house. As Carter was running to get out, he fell on the slick floor, but quickly bounced up and continued to the exit and he, Jones and I retreated. While leaving the house, Jones and Carter returned fire. I was the only one who DID NOT return fire because it was not feasibly safe to do so given I would have had to shoot past my partners. A perimeter was set up, and it became a SWAT scene. The most important thing was that the three of us made it out together unharmed. After hours of negotiations, SWAT sent the robot into the house, and the suspect was found dead inside the bedroom. He turned the AR-15 on himself and died from a self-inflicted gunshot wound. We had to complete walkthroughs of the scene talked to Homicide to complete statements with our recollection of the scene. There were video monitors inside the room where the suspect was, which meant that he could see exactly where he was shooting.

We did not have to report the next day to work

due to it being so late when we finished but were expected back to work the very next shift. This was a traumatic experience because not only did the individual attempt to harm three police officers, but he also ended up taking his own life. We had no real-time away to deal with the trauma, and such was the life of a Harris County Sheriff Deputy. Working the day shift, I learned a lot from the other deputies I worked with. Deputies like Cheatham, Vaugn, Lewis, Leal, and Harris were all very helpful to me learning the ropes. I felt great about my responsibilities, as I was working to serve and protect my community.

While crime was one significant aspect of the job I swore to, nothing could ever have prepared me for the natural disaster I was about to experience as a deputy. Hurricane Harvey was something I will never forget. I remember walking in water chest-deep, and I'm 6'3". Through the darkest hours of the night and early morning during heavy rainfall and standing water, we pulled people out of flooded cars and houses to take them to safety. People cussed us out for taking them out of their flooded homes. Though it felt like a thankless job at times, it was an experience I will never forget. This natural disaster taught me a lot about the difference that peace officers and first responders can make in a trying time such as this. Another memorable call I remember responding to was a shooting in the Haverstock Hills Apartments. The call slip read that a teenager was shot at point-blank range. I arrived first and realized it was on the third floor. As I was running up the stairs, a lady who looked familiar was staring at me. I said to myself, "I know her," but I did not have the time at the moment to stop to figure it out. I walked into the apartment, blood was everywhere, and I saw a young black male bleeding profusely from his leg. As I walked closer, I recognized him!!!!!!!!! The lady started yelling, "PATRICK!!!!! THAT'S MR. BREWER!!! TELL HIM WHAT HAPPENED!" I taught Patrick in 3rd Grade. The lady on the stairs was his mother. He was the student I used to tell, "I am hard on you now, so the police won't have to deal with you later." So many emotions rushed through me at that moment, but I didn't have a minute to think about that because Patrick was bleeding out. I grabbed his wound and applied as much pressure to it as I could. I remember him saying, "Mr. Brewer, you're hurting me!" My response to him was, "I know Patrick, but I'm trying to stop you from bleeding." EMS came soon after and took control of his treatment and transported him to the hospital. The EMS medic told me on the way out that had I not stopped the bleeding; he would have bled out and would not have survived as a result of the wound. I was filled with emotions as they left, but that's what I signed up for, to serve and protect my community. Here was this kid I taught in 3rd grade and was able to save his life from a gunshot wound years later. I wanted to protect and save lives, period!

While working as a police officer, I took a part-time job at Holbrook Elementary in Cypress Fairbanks ISD doing traffic control. I started to develop a good rapport with the faculty and staff. Ms. Garcia, who was the principal, and Ms. Handsborough, who was the behavior interventionist, were two people I communicated with daily. This was a natural element for me since I was a former elementary school teacher. I enjoyed talking to kids at school. One day, I went to sign in for my job assignment, and I stepped back into the office to speak to Principal Garcia and see if there were any traffic concerns. As I did that, I heard what sounded like a little kid yelling, screaming, and throwing a major tantrum. I walked in the room and saw the smallest, cutest curly-haired little girl throwing an all-out fit. I began to talk her in a low, even tone, and she quickly calmed down. Based on our conversation, she was throwing a tantrum because her teacher had told her no, and she did not like to hear the word no. It was the cutest thing ever. This interaction meant a lot to me because when I left law enforcement, I was worried that I would not be able to impact kids directly. Well, this was the beginning of a new friendship. From that moment until the end of the school year, I got parent permission, and I regularly mentored this friend and made it a point to touch base with her daily. This relationship inspired the behavior interventionist to write a children's book based on my interaction with my mentee titled **Officer B and Me** in which a traffic and safety officer named Officer B, helped a little kindergarten student learn to accept no from her parents and teachers. I was so honored and excited about this. Though I had received many accolades in my life, this truly made me proud. Positively impacting kids in any way, shape, or form was at the heart of who I was as a person. Inspiring this book was another way that I could do this. Pam and I became good friends over time, and she wrote a second book titled **Be Bully Free with Officer B**. In this book, Officer B helped students navigate their classroom to be bully-free. Protecting the community as well as continuing to be able to impact the lives of children made me feel like I was honoring my commitment to my purpose.

Overtime-March 22, 2018

On March 22, 2018, my morning started like a typical morning before leaving home. I ate breakfast, played with Jett (my dog), and left to start my shift. The shift on this day began a little differently. I spent the first couple of hours having my body camera docking station installed in my patrol vehicle. I didn't like to be out of service for long due to our shift always being shorthanded. The process took a couple of hours, which did give me time to work on reports, so I was thankful for that.

After leaving the installer, I placed my body camera on the docking station inside of the vehicle, so I could finally get a reasonable charge on it. While driving back to the district, I remembered I hadn't taken my daily blood pressure medicine. Being that I lived in the area that I patrolled, it was no big deal to run inside the house and take it. I arrived at my house, took medicine, and was headed back to my assigned patrol beat. I left home and traveled south on Imperial Valley. There were a couple of tow slips and citations I had written on the previous shift that needed to be turned in at the station. As I approached Rankin, thinking of turning left to go to the station, I decided I had been out of service long enough, and the other members of my shift needed my support, so I decided to hand the paperwork in later, and headed to my assigned beat. I continued south on Imperial Valley and proceeded through the Greenspoint area, which is patrolled by HPD. As I approached Greens Road, the traffic was heavy due to cars stopped in the middle of the street. As I got closer, I observed a black male, approximately 6 feet tall in the middle of the road with his pants down around his ankles, beating on the hood of a light-colored car with two closed fists, while yelling and screaming. This was the reason for the traffic jam because everyone was watching. I quickly identified the behavior as "excited delirium," which is a state in which a person under the influence of PCP, or wet which is the street name, develops supernatural strength, extreme pain tolerance, and undeniable stamina. In my previous experience with individuals under the influence of this drug, tasers were ineffective.

While moving closer to the disturbance, but still in my patrol vehicle, I quickly recalled the last time I encountered someone on PCP and how it took four deputies to subdue the individual. During that encounter, I vividly remembered the suspect had been tased numerous times, but that it was ineffective. Recalling it required two injections from EMS to help us gain control of the individual, I thought about how to approach the situation. I then noticed the driver of the vehicle that was being beaten on exit his car to confront the suspect. I felt the driver's life was in danger and that he didn't know how dangerous this man was. I quickly exited my vehicle as the driver pushed the suspect. I yelled, "HEY! LET ME SEE YOUR HANDS", to get the attention of the man who was in the street beating on cars and causing the disturbance. The suspect then turned towards me and pointed at me. He then started to walk in my direction. I felt as though him pointing at me was his acknowledgment of who I was as an officer of the law. I stood in a squatted ready position with my duty weapon pointed at the suspect. He continued to move swiftly towards me while I attempted to create distance by retreating and continuing to give commands to get on the ground. "GET ON THE GROUND! GET ON THE GROUND! GET DOWN MAN, GET ON THE GROUND, I WILL SHOOT YOUR ASS MAN, GET ON THE GROUND."

I loudly yelled those commands while backing up in and out of traffic at this intersection. I remember hearing people around me, laughing and making comments about the man's erratic behavior. The suspect's eyes were bloodshot red, his mouth was foaming, and he continued to advance towards me, all the while mumbling. I moved right, he moved left, tracking my every step.

While retreating, I knew I needed to make a decision because I was backing up in an unsafe environment with no help from fellow officers. Things happened so fast; I didn't have time to let dispatch know where I was or to get back up. I was truly alone. As I continued to retreat, the suspect continued to advance on me in an aggressive manner getting closer and closer. In my mind, I kept thinking, "Make a decision Cam, make a decision." Fearing for my life and the lives of the individuals nearby, I pulled the trigger ONE TIME, hitting the suspect in the stomach. As the suspect slowly fell to the ground, I holstered my weapon, began to cuff him and started to render aid. While praying for him to be okay, I suddenly heard in my ear, "Hey! Check on David 27!" I forgot I was talking to another deputy on my Bluetooth before seeing this suspect in the middle of the street hitting cars. The dispatch came over the air and said, "42David27 checking on you." I then answered, "David 27, shots fired, roll me EMS and more units, I'm at the intersection of Imperial Valley and Greens Road."

The male whose car was being hit by the suspect was standing there as I was rendering aid and said he would be in the parking lot because he saw everything. As Deputy Jones arrived first on the scene, I told him to talk to the guy in the parking lot to get his information. Deputy Jones told me not to say another word and to get into one of the cars and out of the public view. Deputy Jones went to locate the witness, but he had left the scene. Other deputies showed up to secure the scene. I sat helplessly inside of another patrol car in total shock. I could not believe this happened and continued to pray for the suspect. EMS arrived and took the suspect to the hospital. While in a state of shock, I remember people coming to the car to ask if I was ok. I sat there emotionless and just nodded my head. Soon, I heard a deputy get on the radio and say, "One confirmed.."

As I dropped my head in total disbelief, I realized that my life would change forever. My heart hurt so bad, and the feeling was overwhelming. I replayed the incident over and over in my head and kept saying out loud, "Why didn't he just stop, why didn't he just get on the ground as I said?" I knew based on his actions; he was high on PCP.

All of the signs were there. I was devastated but felt confident in what I saw and my efforts. I could NOT take a chance of this individual overpowering me and taking my gun. There were too many people's lives at stake if that were to happen. All of those thoughts and the fact that I took someone's life tore me apart. While waiting in the car, two men approached the vehicle and told me they were my legal representation and to not talk to anyone else without them present. I was informed that due to the location of the shooting, the Houston Police Department (HPD)would be handling the case. I was then taken to the Houston Forensics vehicle so they could take my duty weapon to check the ballistics. They checked every magazine and counted every round to see what I had left. I advised them I took one shot. I was next taken to do a walk-through of the incident. A walk-through is where you explain the entire scene and your actions. Homicide Detectives surrounded me from HPD and my agency, Harris County Sheriff's Office (HCSO). Also, in attendance were Harris County District Attorneys and other high-ranking individuals from both agencies. After the walkthrough, I was taken by my lawyers to HPD Homicide located in downtown Houston. There I provided my statement of the facts and

circumstances surrounding the shooting.
The Homicide detective from HPD informed me that the suspect had just lost his two children a couple of years ago and that she was the lead detective on that case as well. This, of course, made me feel worse, but I was even more concerned about the chances that this same detective was handling my case. I spent approximately three hours there dealing with statements and other necessary paperwork. I was given a ride back to my car. Still, in a daze, I drove myself home. I knew that I was now a part of the narrative sweeping the nation, police officers shooting black men, and I wished from the bottom of my heart that I was never affiliated with this massive 'trend.' While I do not agree with many shootings that occur, who am I to judge?

Walking in my house, I felt hurt, confused, and scared. I went to Jett's kennel, let him out, and instead of him walking to the back door, he climbed in my lap while I sat down. He knew what I was feeling. He knew I was hurt. This had to be the hardest day of my life.

Double Overtime-
Justice Served?

I spent a few weeks on administrative leave. I was instructed to see a counselor through our Employee Assistance Program. Following that treatment, I was transferred from patrol deputy to desk cop. The Patrol Major advised me that I was not in trouble, that this was to protect me from being in the community due to a large number of police shootings.

Being reassigned to desk cop was very different for me. While I was reassured that I wasn't in trouble, it felt like I was. I was not allowed to work extra jobs. I had no physical interaction with the public. I was happy to be still employed and started to embrace the role and find ways to be effective and efficient.

While on desk duty for less than a week, I got a call to go to our Internal Affairs Division (IAD) to give my statement to them. I spent approximately two hours explaining the circumstances of the case. I was questioned heavily regarding the incident. I felt well prepared and organized with my thoughts. This was not about preparation, but it was more about articulation. The situation was cut and dry: I saw a man in the middle of the street with his pants down banging on someone's car and acting erratically. He was then in a physical confrontation with another man, which put that citizen in grave danger since I suspected the man with the erratic behavior was under the influence of PCP, and I knew a Taser would not work on him. Those facts did not change.

I had several meetings with my lawyers, who informed me they felt I would not only lose my job but that I would get indicted as well. I had no logical understanding of why I would lose my job or even be indicted. I continued to maintain that I acted based upon my past experiences, coupled with training. The next day, I received a call telling me that I needed to report to the Harris County Sheriff's Department main office. My sergeant advised that this wasn't a good sign.

I arrived at the Harris County Sheriff's Department main office, and I was met by the patrol major. The major told me that based on the information provided from the investigation of the shooting, I was being terminated effective immediately for unreasonable use of force and failure to notify dispatch before acting in a police manner. I was floored and could not believe this was happening to me. I asked, "Did anything I said in my statements make sense?" He replied, "We are not going to hold court in my office." I could not believe this was happening to me. So not only was I dealing with taking a human life but now I was losing my career, all of this while serving and protecting my community. I walked out of the office and contacted my lawyer. He instructed me to come to his office. At his office, I was advised the termination was planned and would be on the 5:00 news as the press release was already done. I was terminated just after 4:30 in the afternoon. I felt like they did this to appease the family and a movement, without consideration for the facts. None of this was fair to me, considering I have NEVER been in trouble or written up for the use of force.

A few days later, I was informed that the family was suing me for twenty-five million dollars as part of a wrongful death lawsuit. They cited "racial discrimination" as the basis for the lawsuit. The same civil rights activist who represented Trayvon Martin was representing this family.

Harris County retained a civil lawyer to defend me. Not as a favor to me of course, but they knew that if I got sued, they would be next to in a lawsuit. What worried me was the fact that the news released my home address as a part of the lawsuit. So not only was this case in the media, but the fact that I lived three minutes from the shooting was very troubling for me. This left me on edge. I felt as though at any time, people could come up to my house, and this caused me a lot of anxiety.

A few weeks later, my civil lawyer advised me that the toxicology report came back from the suspect and that he had "high levels of PCP" in his system!!!! I was CORRECT! I knew he was high on PCP, and my training and experience proved that tasers don't work on people under the influence of PCP. I was relieved. The feeling of being confident in what I saw and it being proved to be correct made me feel good. Things were finally starting to turn around for me, right? No. That wasn't the case. The results came back just before my meeting with the Sheriff for me to appeal my termination and attempt to be reinstated. My lawyer presented the toxicology evidence, and the Sheriff still upheld his decision. He said I should have continued to back up until help arrived. He did not see the toxicology report as enough evidence to reinstate me. This hurt me because I knew the suspect was high on PCP, and the toxicology report confirmed it. How can they say "unreasonable use of force" on someone high on PCP? I didn't understand it at all.

Meanwhile, I was being crucified in the media for not "following my training." This did not make sense to me at all. No one would hire me due to the open or pending case as I was still waiting for the case to go before the grand jury. I was truly having a hard time riding this emotional rollercoaster.

Deciding what to do next was easy for me. I completed 150 hours of course work to renew my Texas Teacher Certification while I was unemployed over the next few months. The day I completed the renewal, I had an interview for a 3rd-grade position. This was fate in my eyes, back in the classroom, and this was the 'sign' that this was where I needed to be, right?

I interviewed well and felt great about the chances. The principal seemed impressed by me, and things looked great. I left the interview and went home still hopeful from the day's events. Later that afternoon, my feelings of hope had dissipated. I received a phone call from the principal I had interviewed earlier. She told me as much as she wanted to hire me, she could not do so with the case still pending a grand jury decision. She explained that she googled my name, and the shooting came up. I was upset and tried to convince her that I was innocent, but, it wasn't enough. She told me to come back when this was over. She added, "If I don't have a position for you when this is over, I will recommend you to any school in the district." That was nice of her, but it didn't soften the blow. I gratefully thanked her for her time. Being passed over for jobs happened three more times for decent-paying jobs. They would be ready to hire me, google me, and then withdraw. There was no way I could work a decent job with this case pending. My only hope was to make it until the grand jury met. I felt that all would go away after the grand jury decision. Inevitably, when the grand jury received the information regarding the case, they would see my side. The fact that I gave over ten commands to get on the ground, my backing up the entire time, and the toxicology report showing he was high on PCP, there is no way I would get indicted. I was confident I would be no-billed.

Soon after, I was at a very low point in my life. I started to feel as though life was not worth living anymore. I wanted to die. I was confused, hurt, scared, and anxious. While seeing my counselor, I didn't feel as though I was getting any relief or comfort. My counselor referred me to the

Memorial Hermann Crisis Center. Though it was hard, I knew it was something I needed to do. I went to the Crisis Center and was formally diagnosed with PTSD and depression. I expressed that I could not sleep and was worried about unknown people driving by my house. The psychiatrist prescribed me Zoloft for my mood, and Seroquel to help me sleep. I hated the way the medicine made me feel, but I had to take it. It was necessary for my mental stability.

On October 18th, I received a call from my lawyer out of the blue saying let's have lunch. I found this rather odd and knew it was more to the 'lunch.' We met at Salt Grass Steakhouse, but I was far from hungry. During lunch, he proceeded to tell me the grand jury was going to meet on October 25th, which was the following Thursday. I was immediately sick to my stomach because the time had finally arrived. He showed me the packet prepared for the grand jury to read regarding the case. I was very confident about what I read and felt it was a great representation of what happened. The packet was comprehensive and well organized. The packet outlined the incident; it explained my actions and cited Supreme Court cases to support my actions. The United States Supreme Court gives officers leeway in these situations because of the split second, "life and death" decisions that their profession requires them to make. In Graham v. Connor, 490 U.S. 386, (1989), the United States Supreme Court said that "the reasonableness of a particular use of force must be judged from the perspective of a reasonable officer on the scene, rather than with the 20/20 vision of hindsight". The Court also said that "The calculus of reasonableness must embody allowance for the fact that police officers are often forced to make split-second judgments – in circumstances that are tense, uncertain, and rapidly evolving – about the amount of force that is necessary. The Supreme Court went on to say that in deciding whether the force that a police officer used was reasonable, we must look at the circumstances known to that particular police officer at the time that the force was used. My agency's policy manual even supported me as it relates to the use of force. This standard is also quoted in the Harris County Sheriff's Office policy manual related to uses of force. Section 9.51 of the Texas Penal Code is the state law that says when a peace officer may use deadly force to make an arrest. It states: "A peace officer is justified in using deadly force against another when and to the degree the peace officer reasonably believes the deadly force is immediately necessary to make an arrest, or to prevent escape after arrest, if the force would have been justified under Subsection (a) and: the actor reasonably believes there is a substantial risk that the person to be arrested will cause death or serious bodily harm (Emphasis added) Texas Penal Code 9.51 (c) (2).

Further, "There is no duty to retreat before using deadly force justified in Subsection (c) or (d)." (Emphasis added) Texas Penal Code 9.51 (e).

The night before the grand jury, I was a nervous, anxious wreck. I couldn't sleep as I just wanted this over. All along, I felt like if they just heard my side of the story, they would understand, and I would not be indicted. The only disturbing thing was the fact of how much politics play a role in these types of decisions, and neither my lawyer nor myself was allowed to be in there. It was indeed out of my hands. All I could do was say my prayers and leave it up to God. The next morning, I woke up with no appetite and just wanted the day to be over. I received a text message from my lawyer at around 9 am advising me I was first on the docket. I was nervous because my fate would be decided sooner than later. My attempt to stay busy and do chores around the house wasn't enough to keep my mind occupied. The suspense was tearing me up.

Finally, my phone rang, and I just looked at it. As it continued to ring, I finally answered and said, "Hello." My lawyer, on the other end, said, "Well...bad news...you were indicted." I almost dropped the phone. My heart sank, and I felt numb. I just kept asking, "How?" Of course, he had no answers for me. He then told me he would call me back with my instructions on my next steps.

I hung up with him and began to contact my family and friends to let them know of the outcome. I was being charged with Aggravated Assault by a Public Service and would be facing 5-99 years or life in prison. I broke down and cried the first time in a long time. I was overwhelmed with hurt and had no idea what was next.

Soon after, the District Attorney held a press conference where she announced the charges against me. The way she stood there like she had won a gold medal was heart-wrenching. Hearing her make the comment, "In Texas, there is more than one way to skin a cat," was demoralizing. She mentioned this was the first time an on-duty deputy was indicted in 15 years or so years. Her giving statistics for "unarmed black men being killed" was a total slap in my face because, in my eyes, this case was different from many of the others. In front of the cameras, she painted a tainted picture that I responded to a mental health call and killed an unarmed, innocent black man. This was indeed about politics, and I was being offered as the sacrificial lamb. Had I jumped out of my police vehicle and just started shooting, that would be one thing. If after one of the several commands I gave the suspect and he got on the ground, and I shot, that would be one thing. If he would have just stopped and I shot, that would be one thing. With all the people standing around, had one person said, "Wait, that's my uncle, cousin, brother, let me get him." I would have allowed it. NONE of those things happened. I was backing up the entire time. I gave loud commands as I pointed my weapon at him, and he decided to advance aggressively on a police officer who had his duty weapon drawn, giving him several, specific commands.

Hearing the District Attorney report that I responded to a mental health call and shot down an innocent, unarmed black man who was obviously in a crisis was the farthest from the truth. I could not believe that this is how the situation was being portrayed. It was apparent that the Grand Jury packet that was put together was not considered. I knew they didn't look at my side; they couldn't have. In my opinion, this was one-sided. Not only was my lawyer not allowed to be there for the grand jury to represent me, but my side was never heard. That was clear. The media portrayed me as a savage beast who defied all training and was a reckless rogue cop. They created a "one-sided" narrative. It truly damaged my spirit. If a call had gone out, it was in HPD's jurisdiction. I worked for the Harris County Sheriff's Office, so even if I were dispatched to a call, it would never have been at that particular intersection. The talk of this person being a mental health patient wasn't an accurate fact either. The suspect was NEVER formally diagnosed with a mental illness. Finally, him being characterized as an "innocent person" was a manipulation of the facts.

I noticed him on the scene banging on the hood of cars in the middle of the street with his pants down high on PCP. When does that add up to being innocent? With that being said, I was being charged with a crime. Justice served??

I was advised that my case was being transferred

to another lawyer who would represent me following the indictment. Honestly, I didn't expect this, so I was not prepared. My new lawyer called and introduced himself to me. He advised me that he was trying to find out how much my bond amount was and where I needed to go. He explained that he was trying to get the amount reduced because he knew I hadn't worked a regular job since being terminated in April. I was told to try to get rest, and we would talk in the morning. I spoke to a close college friend who loaned me two thousand dollars to help me with the bond. I will forever be indebted to her and her family for not wanting to see me in jail and helping me at the drop of a hat.

The next morning, I was given my lawyer's address and headed his way to meet to discuss the case. After the meeting, I was given a ride to the bail bondsman who charged me one thousand five hundred dollars for my bond of fifteen thousand dollars. There are no words to describe that moment. I had never experienced this side of the law. Dealing with having to pay a bond and turning myself in was nothing I had ever wanted to experience personally. After paying the bail bondsman, they took me to the Harris County Jail to complete the booking process. Going through a metal detector and past the Probable Cause courtroom to the AFIS (fingerprinting station) was disheartening.

I remember thinking, "Wow, I was the one fingerprinting the "bad guy," now I'm the one being fingerprinted." The deputy took my mugshot and took my fingerprints. Once he was done, I was allowed to go back to the front office to wait for my ride. I was granted this courtesy due to me being a police officer. I was picked up and taken back to my lawyer's office by the bail bondsman. I did not meet with him when I returned. I was told to go home, and we would meet the following week.

I spent the next few weeks in a dark place. I wanted to be alone. Nikki, my sister, wasn't having that. Though she respected my space, she checked on me regularly. Between her and Charles, I was able to "somewhat" express my emotions. It was more helpful talking to someone who had a good understanding. Charles is ex-military and cop. That meant a lot to me. His support at that critical moment truly helped me through some waters that were so difficult for me to navigate.

I had to find ways to cope; I was miserable most days and being an emotional eater, I felt myself becoming quite "fluffy." I was able to reconnect with my old friend/trainer Anthony, who assisted me with getting involved with a workout program. He put me in touch with Josh, a Camp Gladiator trainer. This opportunity was a Godsend. Josh welcomed me with open arms. He helped me get out of that dark place by working patiently with me to lose weight. Josh changed my life, and I am forever indebted to him. He didn't judge me; he just worked with me, understanding my situation. He provided me with meal plans, home workouts, as well as group workouts. Josh believed in my ability to get back in shape and pushed me like no other. He helped me find something positive to focus on my health. Without good health, I couldn't fight for my life. I also enrolled in a master's program at the University of Houston Downtown working towards a Master's Degree in Security Management (which deals with corporate security).

Still not working, my family and friends continued to bless me spiritually and financially. I would have probably lost my house had it not been for the support of these guys. Things were rough, but I was happy to have positive people surrounding me. Nikki (my sister) is like the "mother" of my siblings. While she understood me being in a dark place, she never let me stay there. Jimmy knew how to give me the space I needed and check on me regularly. Brian called to check on me often as well.

These were trying times I faced, but something that truly touched me and reminded me of my faith in humanity was a call I received one weekend. My old student Devon and his mother Ms. Wallace contacted me and wanted to have lunch. I met them at their house and rode with them. We got to lunch, and everything was surreal to me. Devon was the student I mentioned earlier about how hard we worked to get him where he needed to be. Here we were having an adult conversation about life. We reminisced on the old days, and that made me feel good. I was so proud of who he had become, twenty years old now, working a good job, and he even bought lunch. Ms. Wallace had continued to do amazing things with him. When lunch was over, he gave me a gift bag before we left. I opened it when I got home. I cried. The bag contained the book **The Purpose Driven Life**, a favorite teacher mug, a beautiful piece of artwork, a book with inspirational scriptures, an art block with a spiritual quote on it, and cash. This touched me, and it was evident to me that my life mattered to Devon. His actions gave me renewed hope.

While there were flickers of hope during this time, there were serious issues that confronted my life. Mental health is very serious. It only takes one situation that can significantly alter your life. I think that as a community (African Americans), we shrug off all the symptoms and make light of it. Mental health is real, and it needs to be addressed. I went from taking a simple blood pressure pill a day and ibuprofen for pain as needed, to taking over ten pills a day.

Post-traumatic stress disorder and depression require a lot of attention and treatment. Along with PTSD comes anxiety and other related issues. I didn't want to accept that this was my official diagnosis at first, but when I no longer wanted to live, I knew this was not something that would go away. Since being diagnosed, I have taken the following medications: Lunesta, Temazepam, Seroquel, Xanax, Zoloft, Trazodone, Vanspar, and Sertraline. Initially, I started counseling through my Employee Assistance Program (EAP). That counselor referred me to a Mental Health Crisis Center, where I was formally diagnosed. I was referred to the St. Hope Foundation for services. Finally, from there, I was referred to Harris Health. I enrolled in Cognitive Process Therapy (CPT) where I worked one on one with a therapist to assist me in finding effective ways to help me cope with this traumatic experience. I have found that therapy, coupled with the right medication, has placed me on the path to regaining my life. This has been an unbelievable journey that by far, is not over yet. I know now that this is real. If you have suffered something significant in your life that you are struggling to come to grips with, PLEASE talk to someone. I have seen both sides of the spectrum now. I went from being the one taking people to mental health facilities, to checking myself into one. Everyone goes through tough times in life; this is MY story. I want you to hear it from me. I started in life just wanting to conquer the world. I had the ambition to tackle any obstacle that came my way. After going through this, I have experienced so much emotional trauma and have felt I would rather be dead. It has been the equivalent of going from 0 to 100 and then back down to 0. I can now say I have been there.

The anxiety of the trial approaching started to get the best of me. Without God's blessings and the support of family and friends, I would not have been able to hold on. It was so stressful not knowing how bills would be paid, but God always came through. The perfect example is my mom moved in with me to help me with my bills.

Throughout this uncertainty, I picked up things to do, like learning to bowl, working out, and going back to school. I looked for anything positive and productive to take my mind off of facing life in prison. The anxiety only heightened as I awaited the trial. It was like sitting and watching paint dry. I couldn't understand it. The prosecution was in such a hurry to indict me, but time after time they reset the case, ultimately pushing it back further and further. The shooting occurred on March 22, 2018, I was indicted on October 24, 2018, and the trial date was initially set for July 8, 2019. The date then changed to July 22, 2019. On July 22nd, I got a call from my lawyers alerting me that there was a story to be aired that day regarding the trial and the prosecution's attempt to ask for another continuance. Initially, my court appearances were waived until trial. Due to the circumstances of the case, and how things were moving, there was a hearing the following day. My lawyers advised me to attend to show the judge that I was ready for trial. I waited outside the courtroom for my lawyers to meet me. The wait seemed as though it took forever. I didn't understand any of this; I just didn't. If the indictment was done after looking at ALL of the facts in the case, what did the prosecution have to gain from continuously attempting to reset the case?

Once my attorneys arrived, we went into the courtroom. I sat and watched the prosecutors. They appeared to be scrambling, which made me sick to my stomach. I felt as though they were buying time to come up with a case against me. Court ended with the judge sending the prosecution to obtain specific paperwork to return to him.

My lawyers informed me one of four things would happen. One, the date would get pushed back a day or so due to lack of jurors. Two, the date would possibly get moved back a week. Three, the trial would be reset for a couple of months. Four, the trial would start on July 29th as planned.

There I sat the day before the trial was scheduled to begin. I busied myself doing a lot of things around the house. My Aunt Cookie (from Chicago) and Aunt Rose (from Louisiana) were in town. While they meant well, I was not in a visiting mood.

I was in a place where I wanted to be alone, so I went and ran a few last-minute errands. My favorite daiquiri shop was one of the stops I made to get my signature drink, the Triple Threat. The next stop was Cognac Cigars, where I stopped in and smoked my favorite cigar, the Flathead 770. Once that was finished, I returned to my truck to take a drive around the north side of Houston, and then returned home. Once there, I decided to call it a night. Feeling that it would do no good to pick out a suit for the following day because I would change my mind several times, I decided to head to bed so I would be rested for the next day.

July 29th had finally arrived. I was scared, anxious, and didn't know what to expect. I met my lawyers in a designated location and was escorted into the courtroom. There I stood in front of the judge, listened as the charges against me were formally read, gave a plea of not guilty with deputies standing around in case anything went south during the whole ordeal. Just a crazy thing to experience. I felt numb and remember thinking in my head, "Is this happening?" I went home that evening with a ton of weight on my shoulders. My belief had been once the trial started, I would feel better, but I didn't. I began to feel anxious all over again. I went home and laid down for a while, no real appetite, or wanting to talk to anyone. I just wanted to be left alone.

GAME CLOCK
00:00

Jury selection occurred on Tuesday and Wednesday. I was required to be at the courthouse on Wednesday. My mind was all over the place. This was hard for me to process. In all honesty, I couldn't concentrate while facing life in prison. On the morning of Wednesday, July 31st, I sat in the courtroom, waiting for jury selection to begin. I looked around the courtroom before everyone arrived, and I was SCARED of the unknown. Looking at the prosecutors, I didn't know what to expect — seeing Cameron Brewer vs. The State of Texas on the television monitors was a sobering reality that made me very uneasy. Soon the room was filled with 120 potential jurors that were taken down to twenty. It was hard seeing potential jurors that I know would have been fair get taken out or "struck" for no valid reason.

The first day of the trial seemed unreal. News media cameras were everywhere I went. If I looked up towards the doors, the cameras were there; when I entered or exited the courtroom, they were there. It didn't help any that the decedents family took videos of me as well. I felt like a fish in a glass bowl. There were a lot of technical parts to the trial of which I was not aware. The prosecution didn't give an opening statement to the case. This meant that my defense could not present one. They didn't want all of the facts to come out so fast.

The trial was more stressful than I could have ever imagined. As I sat and listened to the prosecution make a case that I should have done something else got old fast. My defense team was amazing. It was refreshing to hear their rebuttal to the prosecution's arguments and give justifiable reasoning for my actions. This went on for a couple of days. As the trial moved forward, it was apparent that the prosecution was not prepared for the case before them. Even the witnesses for the prosecution were testifying to information that strengthened my defense. There was testimony to the dangers of individuals on PCP and how it would take five to six people to subdue them. In addition to that, other expert witnesses for their side testified that tasers are often ineffective on suspects under the influence of the drug. To me, that was important because the prosecution presented first, the jury heard that information early in the case.

I was amazed at how the entire trial process worked. There were untimely delays, unexpected issues, and a lot of contention between the sides.

All of this occurred while I sat there and wanted all of this to be over. It was painful.

Soon the defense took the floor. Things seemed to move a lot faster during this time, and it was driven home how dangerous people under the influence of PCP can be. I can't tell you how important it was to have a strong defense team that believed in me. My union did an excellent job of supplying me with good people capable of doing great things.

My time had finally come. I could now tell my story. FINALLY!!! The jury got to hear from me. I can't remember a time I was so nervous. As it got closer and closer to my turn to testify, my mouth got more and drier. I remember hearing my lawyer say, "Your honor, the defense calls Cameron Brewer to the witness stand." My heart dropped as I stood up, buttoned my suit coat, and walked to the front of the courtroom to testify. It seemed like I walked a mile to get to the witness stand. At first, I started extremely nervous. I began to calm down as we went on with the testimony. I remember thinking this was the truth, my truth, so I was confident in everything I said. The prosecutor examined me and tried to mix me up to get me to say certain things, and overall make every attempt to make me seem "not credible." I remained calm to the best of my ability. My defense was right there on the spot every time a question was inappropriately worded. My testimony went on for what seemed like hours.

It was finally over, and we were done for the day. I was relieved because "my" story was finally told by "me." I was told there would be two more witnesses on my behalf, and then we would be done. My fate was to be determined on August 8, 2019. That was 504 days from the initial incident.

The following morning, I didn't know how to leave home. I didn't know whether to take extra time cleaning my house, spend more time with Jett (my dog), anything. I was so scared I would never see him or my family again. I took one last look at everything, then turned and headed out the door for the courthouse.

Court started after a long delay. My defense was still presenting the case. The first witness was my ex-wife Catrina. Most people would be concerned about an ex testifying, but I wasn't. I was NEVER aggressive or anything like that towards her. I didn't worry at all about her testimony. She testified, and I appreciated her so much for the truth she shared. Next was Pam, the author of the children's books, **Officer B and Me** and **Be Bully Free with Officer B** that I inspired. She testified to my character as well. Last was another expert who was able to reaffirm that I had no other option.

Closing arguments were next. The prosecution didn't go first and allowed my defense team to close first. They laid everything out there for me and explained to the jury one last time how I was an innocent man. Next was the prosecution, and their last chance to prove me guilty. They continued with the same arguments that I should have tasered him. Even though ALL the information provided said differently. They finished, and my case in the hands of the jury.

The jury went to the back and deliberated on the case. During that time, my lawyers talked to me about the possibility of the potential charges and the sentence I could face with my family surrounding me. Those were some emotional moments, and I broke down at one point. After 30 minutes, which seemed more like hours, there was a double tone sound, which indicated that the jury had reached a decision. My heart raced as my fate had been determined. Everyone rushed into the courtroom. The bailiff went back to get the jury. He returned, and everyone stood up…it was a false alarm, and they made a mistake in the number of tones. I sat back down and was sick to my stomach. The suspense of my life hanging in the balance led me to cry again. I was hurt, scared, and at that point did not know what the outcome would be.

We continued the conversation about the possibilities that were before me, and at one point, I remember Charles, Nikki, Markisha, and Montrae praying over me. This was so hard to deal with, and I was so SCARED. Soon after the prayer, a double tone sounded again…This time it was real; clearly, there was no mistake, and the jury had come back with a verdict. Everyone rushed back into the courtroom. The bailiff went out to get the jury, and they walked into the courtroom. Standing with my lawyers, the judge asked, "Has the jury reached a unanimous decision?" The foreman said, "Yes Your Honor." The judge said, "Read the verdict." I remember my heart was pounding hard and fast, like a drummer beating on a drum as I waited for the words. I felt sick to my stomach. The words of the foreman resonated in my head, "We the jury find the defendant Cameron Brewer ...NOT GUILTY of Aggravated Assault by a Public Servant."

I remember breaking down and crying uncontrollably. I could not believe that it was finally over. I cried so hard because this was so hard and it had finally been decided. I hugged my lawyers, Lisa, Wes, and Ed and thanked them over and over and over again. I remember repeatedly saying, "Thank you, Jesus, thank you so much!" I hugged my family and cried. It was OVER! Words can't begin to explain how I felt at that moment. I was found not guilty! I was JUSTIFIED!!!!!

The Question

After reading this book, now ask yourself this question, "Does his life matter?"

About the Author

Cameron Brewer was born in Chicago, Illinois. He earned a Bachelor's Degree in Criminal Justice from MacMurray College in Jacksonville, Illinois. After graduation, he worked at the Cunningham Children's Home in Urbana, Illinois as well as the Boys and Girls Club in Champaign, Illinois.

Cameron then moved to Houston, Texas to pursue a Master's Degree in Public Administration from Texas Southern University. After earning his master's degree, Cameron began a career as a teacher in Houston's historic Fifth Ward.

Realizing the challenges his students faced to and from school daily, Brewer felt a calling to help to create a safer community and began a career as a police officer. This offered him the opportunity to continue to impact children in many ways, positively. Some of his actions inspired a children's book titled **Officer B and Me**, which told the story of a special relationship he built with a struggling kindergarten student. Brewer has spent a significant part of his adult life serving, mentoring, leading and protecting the lives of others. He firmly believes that individuals across the nation should return to invest their time, talents, and resources into the inner city to strengthen the community.

52146569R00055

Made in the USA
Lexington, KY
09 September 2019